WALL PILATES

WORKOUTS FOR BEGINNERS:

EASY 28-DAY STEP-BY-STEP CHALLENGE

EXERCISES FOR WOMEN AND SENIORS TO IMPROVE FLEXIBILITY
AND TONE, BALANCE YOUR BODY WITH ILLUSTRATED ROUTINES.
EXERCISE CHART AND EXPERT TIPS

By STAN BLAIR

Disclaimer

TABLE OF CONTENTS

«I don't have time!»

I have often heard this sentence from people explaining why they cannot exercise regularly. Once they have listed all their reasons, time always seems to be the leading barrier. After all, to many people, working out is another thing to add to an already extensive to-do list. They have businesses to run, households to maintain, bills to pay, children to school, pets to feed – you get the gist. So, once they have barely made it through these lists, exercise is not another thing they want to add. It often ends up on the back burner, forgotten.

Interestingly, while most people can barely find ten minutes to move their bodies, they binge their favorite shows or play mobile games and level up daily. So, while time might be a common reason, there must be something else barring people from exercising. What else can we add to the list of exercise barriers?

Difficulty! Let's be honest. Much of the reason exercise gets ignored is how hard it looks to someone from the outside looking in. Many think training involves several reps, negligible rest periods, a stringent diet, and a rigid routine. So, no matter how committed someone is to losing weight or staying fit, consistency gets more challenging with each rep. After all, how many people can keep up with hour-long cardio sessions six days a week? – Or consuming 1200 calories a day? Most of these exercise and diet regimens need to be revised. As a result, people often ditch their exercise routines by the second month after they start their practices. It's even worse for people who sign up for exercise programs and end up with trainers who push them more than they can handle. I once had a trainer who seemed intent on making me feel powerless by creating exhausting workouts that would run for two hours-those grueling months almost made me detest exercise. And had I not stopped going to that gym, I would have likely shunned practice for good.

How about gym expenses? Another critical reason people avoid exercise is the cost. Let's not even talk about gym memberships. Instead, look at what most fitness gurus will convince you to buy to start gyming. At the very least, you should have some kind of protein powder, resistance bands, a healthy food subscription, some sports drinks, energy bars from a specific brand – the list goes on. An excited person starting their fitness journey might feel overwhelmed by everything they should seemingly have just to exercise. And we still need to cover the gym clothes and massage services you need to recover. It's a lot! Because of this, many people delay starting exercises as they can use cost as a deterrent.

> *I'm still saving money for sneakers. I don't have enough money to buy protein powder and healthy ingredients for daily smoothies.*

Other good reasons exist for not exercising – bad weather, limited space, boring exercise routines, lack of low-impact options, rigid reps, etc. Do any of these reasons resonate with you? **You are not alone.** Even with the fitness waves on social media, many people still intend to participate in another exercise program. I have heard so many good reasons I could write an entire book on why people do not exercise. But reluctance is usual. After you have been through a rigid program or bought costly gym accessories and have not seen progress, it's easy to start seeing exercising as unachievable. And, like many people, you may decide it's not worth the effort and delay or shun it by coming up with a good reason.

Is Wall Pilates the Right Move?

But what if there was an easier way to get moving without pushing your fitness, cost, space, or time limits? What if you could fall in love with moving your body and did not need to invest in every fitness fad in the industry? Does this sound like a pipedream? Well, there is an alternative that works for everyone! Wall Pilates!

If you've been on FitTok recently, you may have noticed an increased interest in minimalistic yet practical exercises. And that is *precisely* what Wall Pilates offers! Unlike traditional Pilates (which is also fantastic for the body), Wall Pilates incorporates wall exercises for additional resistance and support. These exercises are flexible, easy on the body (even for beginners), and fun! Most importantly, they target the entire body and can sculpt every muscle group. And because they use a balance of cardio and resistance training, you can use these exercises to lose weight and stay fit!

- *Do you have a wall?*
- *Do you have ten free minutes to fit in a quick yet effective and fun exercise?*

Then you've got what it takes to do Wall Pilates! You don't need to invest in gym accessories, prepare a workout room, carve out an hour each day, or have the fitness levels of an athlete. Wall Pilates exercises are simple and effective and are thus perfect for **seniors, men, and women!**

Why? These exercises give you control over how you move your body. You can decide how much resistance to use, which allows you to customize the movements per your experience levels. Thus, whether you are old, young, an expert, a beginner, a sedentary office worker, or an athlete, these exercises are right for you!

My Journey to Exercise Freedom

What makes me an expert in a *seemingly new exercise regimen?* Well, that's just the thing. Wall Pilates is not a new phenomenon! It has been around for decades. However, its popularity in recent years owes to its FitTok presence. But even before this interest wave started, I was on the floor, improving my core strength and flexibility. I had started my fitness journey like most people I meet nowadays. Having grown up chubby, I was not very active in sports in school. But after joining college, the breathlessness after one flight of stairs started getting to me. I wanted to keep up with my peers and needed a solution.

So, I tried almost everything people recommended. I ran, went gluten-free, got a gym membership, did planks, hiked, etc. Each time I tried a new activity, I would stick to it for a few days to months. Then I would binge eat, feel terrible, stop trying, and somewhat give up on fitness – this trend continued for years. But one day, things changed. I discovered I loved floor exercises and often enjoyed these gym sessions more. So, when I stumbled upon a class featuring a Wall Pilates version, I was hooked. The following weeks were some of my best gym moments – the exercises were easy, and I could see and feel the results – unfortunately, the gym shut down, which did not sour my love for Wall Pilates.

I continued practicing arguably one of the most straightforward exercises, toned my body, and fell in love with how I felt after each session. I finally trusted myself to follow through with my promises to myself, results that oozed into other aspects of my life. So I jumped headfirst into learning how to impart Wall Pilates skills to others and combined this with nutrition studies. And more than a decade later, I have the perfect exercise for someone who **wants cheap, easy, and adequate training** – Wall Pilates.

A Newfound Joy in Moving Your Body

How do you feel after working out? According to studies, exercise elicits serotonin, dopamine, and adrenaline. But how many people feel relaxed and happy after working out? While this should be the norm (the high you get after a fun activity), many people leave the gym feeling strained, weak, and down. And who can blame them? Doing non-stop cardio followed by weight training and rigorous cooldown sessions will do that to most people. So, while they sleep better and look great, they do not feel as good as they look. They dread working out and are prone to veering off the track.

Exercise should feel good. You should feel exhilaration before, during, and after the exercise. I like to think of Wall Pilates as a rehab for people who have previously viewed exercise as torture. The simple yet effective movements work for your physical and mental well-being. You feel better, stronger, and happier. And guess what? As this book states, you can start reaping these effects in only 28 days!

Throughout this book, I will guide you on the core principles of Wall Pilates which extend beyond the physical. You will learn how to move your body in a safe yet effective way to transform and sculpt your body. I have included expert tips throughout the chapters to ensure you understand Wall Pilates down to an art. And most importantly, I will impart some integral nutrition principles that will help you fuel your body for the ultimate Wall Pilates workouts.

Are you ready? You've got this!

CHAPTER 1: INTRODUCTION

Sustainability is one of the most complex aspects of any exercise program. Often, people start working out with a goal – to lose weight, to keep fit, to sleep better, to feel better about themselves, etc. But along the way, this goal starts fading as they come to terms with what the exercise regimen requires. Here's an example of a client I will call Mary (*not her real name*).

Mary, a 40-year-old nurse, came to me for help establishing an exercise routine. And as part of my process, I dug into her history. She worked long shifts, followed by hours of taking care of her children and aging parents. By the time she had some free hours, she was so tired that going to the gym felt like a chore. Moreover, she often snacked on candy and fast foods to sustain her energy as she ran her errands. Over time, she had gained a lot of weight, making it harder for her to be good at her job and present in her household.

Like many people, Mary had tried exercising and dieting. But since most of her approaches were unsustainable, she would lose momentum and return to her old habits. She'd been at it since she was 25 and knew no other way to keep fit and be healthy. At the end of her rope, she had come to me. It was either that or surgery, and she was giving it one more try.

Mary is a perfect sample of most of my clients. They have tried unsustainable ways (including the cabbage soup diet) and have yet to get positive results. Furthermore, since these unconventional methods are akin to get-rich-quick schemes, the programs' initial effects soon disappear as the regimens get harder. And eventually, they start thinking that exercise and diet are not sustainable and that they should give up – a story as old as time.

Sustainability in Fitness Goals

When people see me, they cannot think there ever was a time when I was on the heavier side, hated vegetables, and barely worked out. My favorite pastime in high school was going to the store to buy biscuits and candy – I would eat till I felt sick. But nausea and increasing weight did not stall me – I kept eating and sitting until I realized the harm I had done to my body. Not only was I missing out on life, but I was also seeing the doctor more often than I liked. So began my journey to a healthier lifestyle. And along the way, I made many mistakes that I have seen in many people. I needed more sustainable approaches to achieve my goal. Could you be making similar mistakes? Let's have a look:

1. Obsessive Scale Reading

Once, I had a client walk into a session. She wanted to lose weight and already had a figure in mind. Then I asked her one question, «What if you do not lose weight?» She looked at me, shocked for a while, and answered that she could not start a regimen where weight loss was not the goal. But only some people lose weight with exercise – most people lose fat. So, while the number on the scale may seem unchanging, your muscles become more toned and increase. And you end up looking leaner and fitter minus the lost weight. However, if you focus only on weight, you can take advantage of these changes and start sabotaging your results. Weight is not a constant – it changes like the tides, especially for women, due to water level and hormonal changes. So, while I will not ask you to *ditch the scale or ignore your BMI*, consider focusing on how you feel more than what the scale says. Eventually, that weight will drop, as will your waistline and all other metrics you wish to reduce.

2. Undereating or Overeating

Calorie tracking is an excellent way to keep tabs on your nutrition. But it can go wrong when your food intake does not correspond to your energy expenditure. Some people eat such few calories that they barely meet their resting metabolic rate needs. And when you eat at such a level, it's hard to even show up for workouts. It's even worse when you under-eat and still show up to work out as you strain your body significantly. Others overeat. I once met people who thought that working out gave them a free ticket to eat what they wanted. So, they would burn some calories and order fast foods within this perceived *eating window*. Of course, this was not sustainable, and they gained weight instead of losing the extra pounds. What an exciting turn of events! But it's more common than you would think.

3. Overexercising or Underexercising

Here's the big one. Aside from food, how you move also affects your health and fitness levels. And you can perform below par or exceed your threshold. Let's start with the person who barely moves. Granted, you are what you eat; nutrition accounts for 80% of weight loss goals. However, exercising is crucial to your goals when on a weight or fat loss journey. Else, you lose lean muscle mass, and your metabolism decreases. These factors make it easier to regain all the lost weight or fat. Overexercising is also wrong. It stresses your body and could lead to adverse hormonal changes. Thus, the key lies in finding the perfect balance.

4. Not Doing Any Resistance Training

Many women and seniors avoid resistance. Some do it because they do not want to bulk up – hint: you can only build much visible muscle if you lift heavy and increase your protein intake. Even then, it takes years to look like a heavyweight bodybuilder. Others avoid it because it is hard. But resistance training is not all about weights or bands – it can be as easy as pushing your weight off a wall, as I will later show you. And the benefits? – it helps you become stronger, improve your metabolism, and look leaner.

5. Being Unrealistic

What do you expect when you work out? People have varying expectations. But sometimes, the perceived results could be more achievable. For example, some people want to lose ten pounds in ten days. Is that a good goal? Any SMART goal proponent will tell you that this is not doable with exercise alone. You would likely need surgery or to restrict your foods so much that your body starts using its reserves. That's not a good goal. Instead, you should focus on better approaches that do not require sacrificing too much.

What does this mean? If your workout and nutrition guides direct you to strain yourself physically or mentally beyond an acceptable threshold, your approach is not sustainable. But there is an alternative that works for everyone.

THE SUSTAINABLE APPROACH: HOW IS WALL PILATES DIFFERENT?

Creating a sustainable workout program comes down to finding exercises that accomplish the following:

- *They do not drain or harm you mentally or physically,*
- *They are not time-consuming and allow you to have a life outside of working out and tracking calories,*
- *They are fun and celebrate your body's capability instead of undermining what it does,*
- *They work for you at all ages and fitness levels and allow you to embrace active living through all seasons,*
- *They do not require you to adopt unhealthy eating patterns or shun the foods you enjoy,*
- *They help you strengthen your body and enable you to keep up with your errands, and*
- *They inspire confidence and help you feel better about yourself.*

And guess what? Wall Pilates checks all these boxes! **Why?** Movement is part of any healthy *lifestyle.*

The keyword here is lifestyle. Any change in your movement or nutrition should align with your lifestyle goals. Say you want to start exercising two hours a day by running around the neighborhood. Can you do that daily ten years from now? How about twenty? Often, people embark on routines that will not work for the entirety of their lives. And once they quit their initial practices, starting other regimens feels hard because they have lost some hope in the process. If you've ever finished a program, you likely know how hard it is to embrace another one after feeling disappointed with a previous trial.

But not all workouts are short-lived, rigorous, or monotonous. Take Wall Pilates which is a revision of Pilates. Pilates is (and still is) a popular way of exercising to **tone your body and improve your flexibility, posture, and balance.** It relies on **creating resistance** in one body part using other parts. For example, the glute bridge forces your glutes, lower back, and core to work hard while your upper back, neck, and feet provide stability. And just like that, you can enjoy a great workout without equipment.

However, most traditional Pilates workouts have some impediments. For starters, most of them require a machine. As such, people who cannot access the Cadillac, Reformer, or other *equipment* must head to the gym to get a traditional workout. Let's not forget that these workouts thus necessitate ample *space* to house the equipment. Secondly, most traditional Pilates workouts are *complex* and not suitable for beginners. So, many people get scared of even trying as they can already determine that the poses are challenging.

*So, how is Wall Pilates different? This workout is the **perfect foundation for anyone who wants to try Pilates!** Instead of going straight to traditional Pilates workouts, you start by using the wall as your support. And the deal gets even better – you can get excellent training from Wall Pilates which will be just as good as what you would get from traditional Pilates. Bet you never saw that coming!*

As the term implies, you rely on the wall for support and stability. So, you can let go of the fear of falling over when trying the exercises. It is like having a trainer in your home, ensuring you have the correct posture even if you have never been to a gym. The wall also acts as a resistance partner. As you push against it, the resistance forces your core to work harder, effects that ripple through your entire body. And yes, you can get toned muscles from this kind of resistance training. You can also use the workouts to target different muscle groups – abs, glutes, biceps, etc.

Traditional Pilates

Most importantly, Wall Pilates workouts have slow and controlled movements, making them perfect for all fitness levels and ages.

A senior can handle the workouts as well as a teenager – it is a level playing field!

Let's use an example to show how Wall Pilates builds on Pilates to make exercises more achievable.

A Traditional Glute Bridge

The traditional glute bridge requires you to lie flat on your back before bending your knees and planting your feet flat on the ground. You place your hands parallel to your body with the palms facing down before squeezing your abs and glutes and elevating your hips toward the ceiling. As you do this, you should not arch your back but instead focus on creating a straight line between your neck and knees. You hold this position for two to four seconds. Then you lower your hips while crunching your abs and squeezing your glutes as you lie flat on the floor again with your knees bent. Similarly, you elevate your hips, squeeze your glutes and abs to create tension, and attempt another straight line.

The Wall Glute Bridge

The wall glute bridge follows a similar sequence. You lie flat on your back and place your arms parallel to the floor with the palms facing downwards. Then you put your feet on the wall at a 90-degree angle and shoulder-width apart, leaving your thighs perpendicular to the floor. At this position, you squeeze your abs and glutes, elevate your hips to the ceiling, and hold the position for two to four seconds. You then lower your hips before thrusting them upwards again.

Your glutes, core, and thighs feel the effect in both instances. But in the Wall Pilates version, you strain less as your body supports the wall. Thus, even a beginner can hack the movements and target the correct muscle groups. I will discuss its core benefits at length in the following chapters.

EMBRACING WALL PILATES FOR STRENGTH, FLEXIBILITY, AND POSTURE

As mentioned, most workouts (including traditional Pilates) have many drawbacks, especially for seniors and women. Thus, it takes a lot to commit to such exercises as they do not inspire you to keep going, which makes them **unsustainable**. Luckily, Wall Pilates addresses these setbacks in the following ways:

1. Affordability

Many people shy away from exercising because they cannot handle the costs. And as a result, many people think exercising requires spending hundreds of dollars a month. It is something they learn from hearing others complain about the high costs. Or you may get this notion from approaching trainers and gyms that charge high amounts. But that is not the case with Wall Pilates.

While you may need a gym membership or machines to do traditional Pilates, you don't need any equipment with Wall Pilates and can start with a wall – just a wall.

So, essentially, Wall Pilates is complimentary. Many people hack the movements even without a mat!

2. Ease

Have you ever walked into a gym and wondered how you would keep up with the trainer or other gym goers? I have! I once joined a gym, and the trainer would have me walk up and down the stairs with weights. I was new to working out and could barely make it up without the consequences. But looking at the others in my class, I could see that this was a rite of passage they had all experienced – their wide, beckoning eyes said as much.

Wall Pilates was a welcome idea. These movements are low impact and gentle on the body. Most of the time, you lie on the floor or use the wall for support. No jumping or any other exercise makes you dread working out.

So, even if you are a beginner or have reasons to avoid high-impact activities, you still qualify for Wall Pilates.

3. Effectiveness

A good workout equals several hours in the gym. I've read about people who get at least 10k steps daily, an hour in the gym, and some light yoga. But how many people have the time to do this? Most of my clients are short on time. They can barely keep their heads above the water, and including a rigorous exercise routine only makes it harder for them to move their bodies.

Wall Pilates workouts are fast and effective. You can be in and out in under half an hour. And while the exercises may seem short and doable, they are effective. You start feeling the results even before you see them. And within weeks, people can tell something is different about you.

4. All-Roundedness

Only a few exercises work on the whole body. I will give examples of all-rounded activities: walking, cycling, running, dancing, and swimming. But of these, only casual walks, swimming, and light dances are ideal for low-impact exercises. The rest feel tough and can result in injuries. Wall Pilates targets the entire body. Not only will you transform your glutes but your abs, hamstrings, biceps, triceps- everything! You will look like you spend hours at the gym, yet your machine is a wall!

5. Safety

I often hear people going, "No pain, no gain." But how true is this accepted saying? It's a pretty dark way to approach working out. Exercise should be fun and safe. It would be best not to hurt while moving or put yourself in any situation that can result in injury. One looks at gym injury reels and sees how bad they can be. And while some of these result from unavoidable accidents, many are due to straining beyond one's fitness levels.

Wall Pilates exercises are customizable to one's experience levels, making them ideal for people of all ages and fitness levels. You start at the foundation. And block by block, you build your stamina and strength, allowing you to progress to advanced postures.

---

6. Progression

Let's not forget that Wall Pilates is a building stone for traditional Pilates. Once you have mastered your core stability and learned how to use your body weight for resistance, you will have a much easier time at conventional Pilates. Better yet, you can progress in Wall Pilates and get a workout as good as you would have from traditional Pilates!

THE 28-DAY PILATES PROGRAM: WHAT TO EXPECT

Rome was not built in one day – nor will any physical or psychological changes present in just a week of working out. Any workout or nutritional change should be something that can last through the seasons. If you cannot eat below 1200 calories for three decades, don't do it even for a week. If you cannot run a mile each day, you should not embark on running only to quit a few weeks later when the going gets hard.

The key should be to ease into a new routine and adapt it to your life, not vice versa.

I believe in sustainable approaches; doing Wall Pilates is a fantastic way to achieve this balance. They move at your pace, do not constrict what you can eat, and allow you to build a solid foundation in traditional Pilates for better posture, flexibility, and strength. These exercises are also integral to preserving lean muscle mass, enhancing mental well-being, and improving overall balance. You should see your body transform in only 28 days. And the longer you stick to our guide, the longer you can build this rewarding habit to see you through your life.

This program is **easy, practical, and proven to work!** I have compiled the exercises I use to ease beginners into Wall Pilates and Pilates. And the gradual steps will help you feel grounded and confident about each new stage. In the following chapters, I will take you through how Wall Pilates transforms your body, how to perform the exercises, how to better your nutrition, and tips for getting better at the activities.

And in line with our focus, I will teach you how to make Wall Pilates a sustainable addition to your life. It will be so ingrained in your schedule that it will feel effortless – just like any positive routine should feel!

CHAPTER 2: BENEFITS OF WALL PILATES FOR BEGINNERS AND ITS PRINCIPLES

"It's just a class where people stretch and contort their bodies."

That was the response I first got when I showed interest in doing Pilates. My advisor at the time was heavily invested in lifting weights. And he did not understand how people doing Pilates could achieve lean muscle mass, feel invigorated, or even lose weight. But I had had enough of the conventional exercises and was not about to entertain another trainer who would push me to my *limits*. So, I signed up for the class which promised me a new body in a month. After all, the instructor looked like she knew a thing or two about exercising – the abs said it all.

Weeks later, I realized Pilates was not just a class about stretching. I had finally moved some parts I thought were too rigid and could feel as I became limber. I felt lighter, happier, and transformed even though the weight on the scale had not moved much. And I then understood that Pilates had more to offer than I initially thought. It was not just another exercise to push through as I had previously done – this kind of movement would have me returning for more.

So, what about Pilates makes it so great, and why does wall Pilates enable you to reap the most benefits from this incredible movement?

Walking Down the Pilates Memory Lane

My first Pilates session was awkward. I had come from a class where warmups often included burpees and skipping rope for almost half an hour. So, I expected some jumping as the instructor yelled at me to stop holding back and push through the pain. Instead, she walked me through the movement instructions so gently that I was unsure the movements would make any difference. But boy, was I wrong! In minutes, I could feel the burn and could not help but wonder who stumbled on this impactful movement.

And since I have always been curious about exercises, I looked into how Pilates began. The story floored me. It started with a man named Pilates *(shocker)*, whose health challenges in childhood encouraged him to train as a gymnast. The constant training enabled him to grow stronger, alleviating most of his symptoms and increasing his strength and endurance. Moreover, it allowed him to travel the world as part of a performing troupe. But as luck would have it, the First World War broke out when Pilates was in England. And he thus found himself stuck in the Isle of Man. Rather than allow captivity to get the best of him, Pilates studied cats and how their movements allowed them to move swiftly and elegantly. He concluded that a mind-body connection was the answer – humans could be as limber and robust if they trained their minds and bodies. So began his quest to mimic the cats and transform his body to achieve more than he had as a gymnast.

Pilates started stretching using his body weight and eventually used the available equipment to make makeshift stretching machines, allowing him to experiment with more techniques. As a former gymnast, he had an advantage, enabling him to create routines whose

effects were soon visible on his body. Naturally, the other detainees were curious to try the workouts to become stronger and beat the boredom. They practiced with him, learning to use their bodies as support and reaping the fruits of their hard work. And guess what? When the Great Influenza reached the camp, none of the trainees fell sick. If anything, they appeared **stronger** than when they first came the camp! That was enough proof that Pilates was onto something.

Once Pilates left the camp, he eagerly shared his routines with others, eventually moving to Manhattan, where he set up a booming fitness business with his wife. His earlier attempts at makeshift machines allowed him to create the original versions of the Reformer and the Cadillac, which became the standard for Pilates workouts. His programs were so successful at **strengthening bodies and increasing flexibility** that actors, dancers, and other top performers sought his rehabilitation services. And, of course, his fantastic physique drew many from far and near – everyone wanted to see if Pilates workouts were as magical as described. It turns out they were!

As his fame spread, many students turned their passions into careers and opened gyms across other states, enabling many to try Pilates. At first, the interest in Pilates mainly came from dancers and actors who wanted to remain **limber and strong**. But towards the start of the 21st century, people started looking for alternatives to aerobics and weightlifting *(been there, done that)*. Pilates was a welcome answer, allowing people to embrace **bodyweight movements at slower paces.** It was an exercise anyone could hack. And once stars started opening up about their love for Pilates, this once little-known exercise became the go-to for many people who wanted to **lose weight, contour their bodies, gain strength, become flexible, and fall in love with movement** – the list was endless.

Over a century since Pilates introduced this fantastic workout, it continues transforming people mentally, physically, and spiritually. So, what's the secret to this success?

BREAKING DOWN THE PRINCIPLES BEHIND PILATES

I won't lie – Pilates may be gentle, but it is not the most straightforward exercise. It will have you heaving and sweating and grunting. Most of the people in the class will barely hear you as they will also be doing their best to maintain their postures and not fall over. It's funny, a great way to gauge your fitness levels, and challenging enough to pump that adrenaline.

Do you want the master key? Getting better at Pilates is all about mastering its core principles which are also essential in Wall Pilates. What are they?

1. Breathing

Breathing is one of the most essential body functions. Leave alone the fact that breathing keeps us alive. It also contributes to general well-being by calming our nerves. Many people find that deep breathing allows them to ground themselves in situations where stress and anxiety can get the better. Breathing is also integral to focusing better and enables you to avoid distractions. And as a plus, breathing is a great way to engage muscles which is *precisely* what you want when doing Pilates or any other exercise.

Given the importance of breathing, it is at the core of all Pilates workouts. As you embark on any exercise, you must inhale and exhale properly to allow you to focus on your mind-body connection. You should draw enough air to feel it move down to the sides of your rib cage while pushing down the diaphragm. Doing this engages the core muscles and increases your focus on the movement. Then you should exhale sharply by forcing the air out of your lungs such that you feel the diaphragm rise as your abs crunch. You should keep breathing like this throughout all the exercises as it engages your muscles and keeps you focused.

Anytime I ask you to breathe, use this breathing technique to ground you when explaining the movements in the 28-day program. Do not hold your breath. Instead, breathe normally and use some extra force to inhale and exhale such that you feel the changes in your diaphragm and rib cage.

2. Focus

A mind-body connection is not instant. Instead, you must will yourself to be attentive to the movements. Let's use the toe tap as an example. The exercise seems simple to someone watching another perform it. But this exercise requires a lot of concentration. You must breathe in and out as described under the first principle. As you do this, you should ensure your back is flat on the floor while your hands are on your side, with the palms facing the floor. You then bend your knees and plant your soles on the ground. And you start moving one leg up to a 90-degree angle and lowering your foot to gently tap the floor before raising it while focusing on the tension in the abs and crunching them!

Performing any Pilates exercise requires a lot of focus as you see and feel the results if you follow the proper movements. You should know how to position yourself, target muscle groups, and breathe in different positions. Focusing enables your brain to make the connection which eases subsequent attempts. That's why Pilates lovers seem so flawless in their actions – it is all about making that connection, and your brain will do the rest.

3. Control

Do you think you can control your body? Well, here is some news. Besides breathing and focusing on movements, you must control your body during Pilates. But that is easier said than done. For example, when doing a bird dog, you must balance your body and tighten your core before raising alternate legs and arms. Doing this requires controlling your entire body to ensure you target the right muscles and do not fall over. This control is not something you master in one movement. Instead, you build this control by continuously practicing the moves, leaning on greater focus, and breathing at every juncture. Over time, the muscle memory and brain connection kick in, allowing you to flow through sessions like a pro. As you start any of the exercises in this program, I urge you to follow the procedures, as this allows you to master each movement.

4. Relaxation

I know urging you to control your body and following it with relaxation might seem odd. But the only way to fully embrace the mind-body connection is to relax. Often, people show up to workouts feeling stressed or tired. And this diverts their attention as they try to rush through the processes. Doing this makes it hard to follow the correct movements and can harm your progress. While Pilates is a safe and low-impact exercise, it's still a movement, and positioning your body wrong can subject you to injuries. Before the exercises, do deep breathing and focus on what's ahead. It relaxes your muscles and gives you a better chance of flowing through the practice.

5. Alignment

In the past, office workers were most likely to develop back and neck issues because of continuous hunching. But now, the constant use of phones and laptops strains so many necks and backs that almost everyone needs alignment. And what better way to achieve this than Pilates? The concept is simple. Each movement aims to re-align the body in its neutral and natural posture, which is why Pilates instructors have such solid and confident stances. As you move through the exercises, find the correct position that mimics this neutral positioning. For example, you should not arch your back when doing a bridge but instead maintain a straight line between your knees and neck. Getting this positioning right relies on the previous principles – breathing, focus, control, and relaxation.

6. Centering

Have you seen just how strong the cores are in people who do Pilates? But these workouts are not just about having flat stomachs with rock-hard abs. Instead, the centering aspect allows you to connect with your physical, mental, and spiritual senses. The more you focus on your core, the easier it is to tap into your energy and coordinate the other movements. When you should engage your body during the program, it allows you to connect with the **flow of the actions** so that you can perform them in one go.

Movements in Pilates should be swift (almost catlike), and this only happens when you have a centered core. And as you may have guessed, you must rely on the previous principles to hack this fluidity!

IS PILATES THE KEY TO A HEALTHY BODY?

The Great Influenza ravaged many people. Yet none of Pilates' trainees succumbed to the disease. This result left many people wondering if Pilates worked magic. Is it all that? Well, scientific studies over the decades have shown that this routine comes with the following perks:

1. *It is fantastic for posture and flexibility. The Pilates principles enable people to enhance their alignment and regain their natural poses. They also help them become more limber, breathe better, and feel stronger.*

2. *It targets the whole body. While movements often target specific muscle groups, the fluidity between sets allows people to work through their entire bodies. As a result, they experience muscle development and increased strength.*

3. *It embraces everyone. Most people shy away from new workouts because they don't fit their needs. But Pilates does! It is so all-encompassing that it works for all ages and fitness levels, including older adults, pregnant women, and people recovering from injuries!*

4. *It boosts energy. Are you in a slump? Many people are. Pilates helps you move past these blocks by allowing you to center yourself in all aspects, increase your focus, and move your body in ways that open you to more energy.*

5. *It is customizable: Pilates is not a rigid workout. While you should exercise control during the exercises, you can constantly tailor them to your needs. For example, if a glute bridge seems challenging, you can do a bridge instead and still get a fantastic workout.*

Of course, the weight loss is a plus for anyone looking to shed some extra pounds!

WALL PILATES: THE PERFECT FOUNDATION FOR TRADITIONAL PILATES WORKOUTS

Pilates is a great way to move your body, reclaim energy, and align your body. But starting with Pilates workouts is only sometimes doable, especially for beginners needing help mastering the principles. Starting with Wall Pilates allows you to create the least challenging Pilates versions and build your confidence. It also allows you to reap the following benefits:

1. Confidence

Pilates requires a mastery of so many principles that it scares beginners. I would not ask any of my beginner clients to start with a hip twist. This pro exercise is so demanding on the core that many people quit halfway and end up disappointed. Such experiences can bar you from pursuing Pilates as a whole. Wall Pilates allows you to take in the Pilates principles in bits that build your confidence, making it easier to embrace more challenging workouts when ready.

2. Accessibility

Wall Pilates requires just a wall to start. And this eliminates the need to get a gym membership or buy a Pilates workout machine. It saves you time, space, and money. And this makes it an excellent choice for everyone. You can even enjoy a workout at the office, and nobody will be the wiser.

3. Increased Coordination

Pilates requires you to master a mind-body connection. But for many people, this is challenging. Most people spend years working out without such links, e.g., aerobics. So, starting with a traditional Pilates workout may feel intense. You can begin with Wall Pilates which simplifies the connections and allows you to build a solid foundation.

4. Added Strength

The control required in Pilates workouts also hinges on a solid body. So, how can you have your cake and eat it? – By building your endurance through Wall Pilates! The wall provides resistance while your body weight allows you to strengthen your muscles. By the time you get to roll-ups, your core will have the strength to power through any movement.

5. Low Impact

Pilates is a low-impact exercise. But while this may be the case, many people need to start at the lowest impact levels, e.g., older adults at higher risk of injury. Wall Pilates takes machines out of the equation and allows you to align your body slowly, reducing your risk of injury. Moreover, the wall also guides your body from putting undue pressure on weak joints.

6. Added Balance

Doing Wall Pilates gives you a sense of your body's positioning regarding your space. You learn to move safely, making it easier to control your body when the wall is not in the picture.

MOVING YOUR BODY SAFELY FOR LONGEVITY WITH WALL PILATES

Wall Pilates is like training wheels for traditional Pilates. And in a month of doing Wall Pilates, you will be on the fast track to the usual Pilates. But as I have mentioned severally, Wall Pilates can be just as effective as the conventional Pilates workouts, and leveling up is optional. Even so, you may have concerns about starting a new exercise program. These include:

- *Is Wall Pilates rigid? How often must you exercise? Do you have the time to stick to the program?*

- *Must you start limiting your calories and adopting "clean eating?" Should you throw away those candy bars you love so much?*

- *Are the exercises boring and repetitive? Can you customize them?*

- *How soon will you see changes? How can you measure your progress?*

- *Can you suffer injuries? Is fatigue awaiting you?*

- *Will the program take over your life?*

- *Do you need new gym accessories?*

People often talk about intuitive eating (which I lean on when offering nutritional advice), and some of these principles apply to moving your body. The only way to enjoy Wall Pilates or any exercise is to approach it sustainably, which I emphasized in the previous chapter. I have created a program that addresses the concerns above by tapping into different movement needs and nutritional goals, creating a low-impact, core-strengthening program that helps you master Pilates principles.

Earlier, I discussed some reasons people give up on new programs. In the following chapters, I will walk you through how to incorporate Wall Pilates into your life and build a sustainable lifestyle around fun and effective wall-based exercises. Along this line, I will show you how to set realistic goals for your fitness and weight. I will also cover how to stay safe when starting this program, how to tailor your meals to your goals, ways to prevent injuries, sustainable ways to measure your progress, and how to avoid the most common fitness mistakes.

This program does not make Wall Pilates the be-all and end-all of exercises. It is not absolutist, nor will it have you counting calories in every grape you taste. Instead, it focuses on sustainable approaches to health and fitness by introducing all-rounded Pilates principles in gentle and fun exercises. Let's address safety and consistency concerns in the next chapter.

CHAPTER 3:
PREPARING FOR THE 28-DAY CHALLENGE

Failing to plan is planning to fail

While this saying seems simplistic, it is an incredible way to approach multiple life aspects. For example, if you want your business to succeed, you must have a solid business plan for achieving this success. In the same way, if you're going to get fitter, lose weight, sleep better, or even fix your posture, you must plan how you will do it. Otherwise, your aspirations remain just that –dreams! In this section, I will explain how you can set up a practical Wall Pilates workout space, how to set your fitness goals, and how to embark on the 28-day challenge safely. Please read this before commencing the challenge. While the exercises are beginner-friendly, taking precautions is always advisable.

Setting the Tone for Wall Pilates with a Suitable Workout Space

Traditional Pilates studios feature many machines, thus challenging to set up in the home. But Wall Pilates workout spaces are so easy to create that you will not even need help with the process. Moreover, you can set up your area in just a day. Here's how you should go about it:

1. **Choose a suitable space:** Wall Pilates is not a space-demanding exercise. Even so, you should choose the ideal location for your workouts by considering the following factors:

– *How ample is the space? Wall Pilates relies on a wall for the most part, as this offers resistance and support. However, most of the movements require you to stretch your hands and legs. As such, choose a space measuring at least six square feet. It allows you to try the exercises without knocking things over. Plus, if you fall, you know you will not hit a table or anything that might hurt you.*

– *Can you enjoy uninterrupted exercise? Wall Pilates, like traditional Pilates, centers on Pilates principles. You must choose a space to exercise breath control, focus, precision, and mind-body connection without distraction. Some people prefer using the privacy of their bedrooms, others use the area under the stairs, while others can use their living rooms. You can gauge what nook best serves this purpose based on your household. If you have enough space to spare an extra room, you can dedicate it to Wall Pilates.*

– *Does the space have enough ventilation? You should get enough air when doing Wall Pilates, allowing you to focus on your breathing and cool down between sets. Choose bright and airy spaces for this.*

2. Set up your equipment: What do you need for a Wall Pilates workout space? Luckily, you can start with just a wall. But if you want to switch things up a bit, you can always include the accessories below:

– *A yoga mat allows you to exercise floor while enjoying additional support. Getting a carpet if you have suffered injuries before or want to cushion when working out is a good idea.*

– *A candle – some people enjoy working out in candlelight as it helps them focus better on the movements.*

– *Incense – Do you fancy some scents to encourage deep breathing? Consider incense.*

These accessories are optional. If you have a wall, you are good to go and do not need to start breaking the bank to set up your space. The 28-day program focuses more on movement than equipment; you will make it even without these accessories.

3. Create the right ambiance: Many people like working out in the gym because the environment inspires them to get moving. In the same way, your workout space should feel different from the rest of the house to communicate that it's specifically for Wall Pilates. Below are some suggestions you can consider:

– *Paint the wall a different color or use wallpaper to set the tone,*

– *Add a mirror on the adjacent wall to help you watch your form and also create the illusion of a bigger space,*

– *Post your workout schedule or log on to the wall to remind you what to do.*

This step is customizable per your preferences. And you can as well skip it if you wish.

Voila! You're done and can now use the space for Wall Pilates! But what exactly is your goal for undertaking the program? You may already know what you want, e.g., to get stronger. It's time to set and refine your fitness goals to ensure your workouts give you the satisfaction you deserve. Trust me – this is one of the most exciting parts of any program – my clients are often over the moon when we start this process.

Putting the SMART in Fitness Goals

Are your fitness goals realistic? In Chapter One, I mentioned that unrealistic fitness goals were part of the reason most fitness programs fail. After all, if you weigh 300 pounds and want to lose 100 pounds in 3 months, that is not doable in a healthy way. The same goes for someone who barely works out and wants to start running marathons in two months. Before setting up any goal, you must look at where you are and where you want to go. That gap determines how soon you can reach your goal and the best way to get there, which becomes your fitness plan. Let's consider how goals work in Wall Pilates:

Finding the Gap

Wall Pilates is an excellent foundation for Pilates. And the stronger you become, the easier it will be to embark on other exercise routines, including lifting weights. However, it all starts with embracing your fitness levels at the program's start, as these inform your SMART fitness goals. Often, people overestimate their fitness levels and assume they can achieve a lot quickly. But the only way to know is to test yourself using the tests below. Try all of them in the order presented:

Doing a plank

1. The Plank Test: Wall Pilates is fantastic for core strength and stability, making it an excellent method for core strengthening. So, what's your core strength as you start the program? An easy way to gauge your current core strength is to do a plank, as it requires several muscle groups to work together to support this position. And as the burn and trembling start, your endurance and core strength determine how long you can hold the position. Here is how you test yourself:

– *Lie on the ground and elevate yourself to a plank position with your forearms lying on the ground for support. Hold this position for sixty seconds.*

- *Lift your left arm off the ground and hold the plank with your right forearm for fifteen seconds. Lower your left forearm to the ground and lift your right arm for fifteen seconds.*

- *Return to the plank position with your forearms on the ground and lift your left leg for fifteen seconds. Lower the left leg and lift your right leg for fifteen seconds with the left leg on the ground for support.*

- *Return to the original plank position and lift your left arm and right leg off the ground for fifteen seconds. Lower them to the ground and lift your right arm and left leg for fifteen seconds.*

- *Lower your right arm and left leg and return to the plank position for thirty seconds.*

You're done! How did you fair? Each stage you complete amounts to a point. So, if you did all 5, you have exceptional core strength and will likely breeze through the Wall Pilates workouts. But if you scored below 5, Wall Pilates can help you improve your core strength through Pilates principles.

2. **The Push-Up Test:** The second way to gauge your fitness is to do some push-ups. My clients often groan at the suggestion, but push-ups are some of the most effective upper-body exercises. And the more you can do, the stronger and the better you are at control, precision, and alignment. Do these principles sound familiar? How do you think you are fair? Test your push-up levels in the following way:

- *Start at the push-up position and lower your body until your elbows are at a right angle. (You can also do the half push-up post where you hinge your body by being on your knees. This position is more manageable for beginners.) Lift your body back to the push-up place.*

- *Repeat the push-ups as often as possible, ensuring you do not compromise your form. Stop when you can no longer keep going without maintaining neutral alignment.*

Doing a push-up

1. The Wall Sit Test: How strong are your legs, and how much can you endure? This test helps you gauge your lower body strength as follows:

– *Picture an imaginary chair whose back is the wall. Sit on it with your back to the wall and maintain a 90-degree angle between your knees and hip joints.*

– *Start a timer to count the seconds. Keep breathing and pushing your back to the wall and ensure your form does not suffer.*

The scores for women are as follows per the seconds of holding the position: Excellent (46+), Good (36+), Fair (20+), and Poor (<20). Men score as follows: Excellent (76+), Good (58+), Fair (30+), and Poor (<30). Where do you fall?

Doing a wall sit.

The above tests help you gauge your upper, core, and lower body strength. Your scores determine the baseline for your fitness levels and help you set goals. For example, someone with a 15-second wall sit score can improve this to 50 using Wall Pilates. Do not let your scores discourage you – if anything, use them as motivation to set your goals so you can track your progress during the program.

Setting Realistic Goals in Wall Pilates

You have your space and know how fit you are. Let's set some goals before starting the program. Sticking to the schedule is much easier when you know where you're going. Use the steps below:

1. **Acknowledge where you are:** Say you can only hold a plank for ten seconds. That shows that you need to work more on improving your core strength. Note your performance in each test, as you can use the score to determine if you have made progress as the program ensues.

2. **Decide where you want to be:** Some people want to do fifty pushups at a time. Others want to do wall sits for minutes. Understand what matters to you, as this will inform your next steps.

3. **Dig deep for your WHY:** Motivation is a great tool. For example, if you want more upper body strength to play with your children, that's a powerful reason. Each time you work on your goals, you will remember why you're doing so, which makes it easier to be disciplined.

4. **Be SMART:** Dreaming big is not an issue. You can hope to do 100 pushups, yet you can only do 15 currently. That's possible. But how you set the goal matters, which is why you should consider the following factors:

- *Specificity: What's your goal? E.g., you want to lose 50 pounds through Wall Pilates.*

- *Measurable: How will you measure your progress? Saying you want to improve your core strength is not a good start. But stating you wish to do 50-second planks is an excellent description, as it allows you to track your progress over time.*

- *Attainability: Can you achieve the goal? While some plans sound good, they are not attainable. For example, someone who wants to start doing 30 more pushups in five days will likely fail to achieve their goals. Set a plan you can achieve sustainably without compromising your well-being.*

- *Realisticness: Is your goal relevant to your WHY? You should ensure that it matches your purpose, as this affects how disciplined you will be in attaining it.*

- *Timeliness: Have a deadline to achieve your goal, e.g., increase your planking time by 20 seconds within 14 days. This timeline allows you to track your progress to review where you went wrong and amend your approach if you fail to hit the target.*

5. **Break Down Your Goals:** Start with a big goal, e.g., lose ten pounds in two months through Wall Pilates. Then break this down into smaller goals to help you gauge your progress, e.g., five pounds in a month. Creating these KPIs (key performance indicators) makes it easier to achieve your goals because you focus on the next step instead of the entire journey.

6. **Focus on one goal:** The tests may encourage you to target more goals at a time. But here's the thing. Chasing too many dreams reduces your focus on what is most important. Choose the plan that best matches your WHY and work on it first.

Here is an example of a SMART goal: *I can hold a plank for only 12 seconds. I want to increase this time to 40 seconds in 30 days. I will achieve this by following the 28-day Wall Pilates Challenge, which will help me improve my core strength and endurance.*

Have you created a SMART goal? Ensure you have one before starting the program – I cannot emphasize this enough.

Safety Precautions and Warming Up for Wall Pilates Exercises

When people start new exercise programs, they often push themselves a lot, hoping to see the results in days. You've likely seen the memes – people looking for abs after one pushup. But these jokes hold a lot of truth. Many people expect results in days and thus often go hard at any new program. But doing this takes the fun out of the exercise and increases the risk of injuries. Injuries are prevalent where one has a history of injuries, low endurance, imbalanced strength, and low flexibility. And for many beginners and people who lead sedentary lives, these risk factors are high. It's thus essential to abide by safety precautions to ensure your Wall Pilates journey is **sustainable** as follows:

a. *Start slow: The 28-day program builds from a gentle foundation. While you may feel tempted to increase your pace, do not. Short exercises are much safer than prolonged exercises, which can strain your muscles. I have created sets that push your body just enough to set the pace for increased strength and endurance while protecting you from injury. Moreover, the sets target different muscle groups to avoid straining some body parts, which can result in fatigue or injuries. Please follow the program as outlined.*

b. *Mind your posture: Wall Pilates follow specific guidelines on body alignment. You should follow the instructions in the program as they are integral to avoiding injuries.*

49

c. *Use the Pilates guidelines:* During the exercises, you should practice deep breathing, neutral postures, precision, and relaxation. It allows you to flow through the steps and not hurt yourself.

d. *Warm up for at least five minutes before the exercises:* Wall Pilates is low-impact. But before starting the postures, you should warm up your muscles by stretching, running on the spot, or taking a short walk. Doing this reduces the risk of injury and mentally prepares you for the workouts.

e. *Consult your physician:* Most people can start Wall Pilates without adverse effects. But if you have underlying health conditions, you should consult your doctor on whether you can create a new program. Examples include people with heart problems or high blood pressure.

f. *Take your time:* The exercises in the 28-day program allow you to move slowly. Do not rush them. If you feel strained, take a break and return when you feel more energized.

Resting

g. *Fuel your body:* Eat enough calories to sustain your exercises. Even if you have a calorie deficit, ensure you factor in the practices to have enough energy. Otherwise, you will underperform and risk feeling faint, reducing the postures' effectiveness. I have covered more about nutrition in Chapter Six.

h. *Optimize resting between active days or when sick:* Rest is vital for your body to recover It also aids muscle development and is suitable for your mental health. If you have difficulty resting, consider active recovery, which includes stretching your body with minimal impact.

i. *Stay hydrated:* Exercise can dehydrate the body. Thus, find ways to stay hydrated, such as drinking water and tea. You can add fruits to your water to make it taste better. Aim for at least eight glasses of water a day.

j. *Dress for Wall Pilates:* You should wear comfortable clothes when exercising. Aim for breathable and light clothes in the hotter months. And as the weather gets colder, wear heavier clothes to protect yourself from the dropping temperatures.

Most importantly, avoid absolutist thinking where things are either black or white. Allow yourself to listen to your body, break when necessary, and do not push yourself too much. The 28-day program is a marathon and not a sprint. And if you stick to the guidelines above, the changes will show in just weeks. Are you ready? Do you have a SMART plan, a good workout space, and safety precautions in mind? The next chapter walks you through the 28-day program workouts.

CHAPTER 4:
START 28-DAY STEP-BY-STEP WALL PILATES WORKOUTS

Are you ready to get leaner, fitter, more flexible, and improve your posture? The next few weeks can help you achieve these and more goals. Use the safety precautions outlined in previous chapters to ready yourself for each exercise. And most importantly, follow the instructions to ensure you control your movements and not strain your muscles. Let's go!

Week 1 – Foundations of Wall Pilates

This week is about familiarizing yourself with Pilates movements. You start practicing breath control, precision, and alignment, which will help you in the coming weeks. Each workout takes about 20 to 25 minutes.

DAY 1: WALL ROLL DOWN AND SPINE STRETCH

Wall roll-down stretch

Wall Roll Down Spine Stretch

This beginner exercise that targets the abs and shoulders helps you master a spine stretch while working your abs so you can perform more challenging roll-up activities as you progress. Here is how you do it:

1. *Stand next to a wall with your back to the wall, leaving about eight to ten inches of space between your body and the wall.*

2. *Plant your feet firmly on the ground and ensure you feel stable as you maintain a shoulder-width distance between your feet. Place your arms on your side and relax them so they fall against your torso.*

3. *Engage your core by pulling in your abs and relaxing your shoulders to ensure they do not touch your ears. Breathe in and feel the air as it pushes your diaphragm down and your rib cage out, resulting in a broad chest.*

4. *Start exhaling as you move your body downwards from the head to the spine. Feel as you move each vertebra as you push out the air forcefully. Ensure your core remains engaged as you do this so you can feel as the spine lengthens with each roll.*

5. *Allow your arms to follow the movement parallel to your ears but ensure your hips remain against the wall. Do this slowly and feel as the tension releases from your body. Keep rolling down until you cannot do so without moving your hips.*

6. *Inhale at this point as you keep engaging your core and feel the effect. Focus on how your body feels from head to toe. You will likely get a good stretch even in your legs, but you should not feel pain.*

7. *Exhale sharply as you roll up, starting from your lower abs. It would help to use your hips and lower abs to hinge this motion to ensure you target one vertebra at a time. Rolling back up might prompt you to create tension in your shoulders but avoid doing this by relaxing them.*

8. *Come back to the original position without disengaging your abs.*

Repeat the exercise twenty times, ensuring you move slowly with each rep and avoid raising your shoulders or forcing your body to stretch even when it lacks flexibility.

DAY 2: WALL SQUATS AND LEG CIRCLES

Wall Squats

The wall squat, called the devil's chair, is a fantastic beginner exercise targeting the **glutes, calves, and quadriceps.** It helps you build your endurance, allowing you to perform better in challenging Pilates.

1. *Place your back against the wall, leaving a space of about two feet from the wall. Distance your feet at shoulder width and engage your core.*

2. *Lower your body as you move your back against the wall so that your back touches the wall, but your feet remain in place. Do this until you achieve a 90-degree angle between your knees and hips.*

3. *Ensure your knees are above your ankles rather than your toes to allow you to target the right muscle groups and avoid straining your knees.*

4. *Maintain this position with your back against the wall. You will feel the burn and might even start shaking. But hold it for twenty seconds.*

5. *Return to the original position by sliding you back up (not down) the wall and rest for thirty seconds. Sliding up ensures you complete the exercise by putting more pressure on your glutes.*

6. *Lower your body again and add five to ten seconds to the original wall squat time. Then come back up again.*

Do this exercise five times, ensuring your thighs are at a 90-degree angle and your weight is on your ankles?

Leg Circles

These exercises target your **glutes and thighs**, help you build endurance, and are ideal for toning your legs. You don't need any equipment and can perform them as follows:

1. *Stand with your feet shoulder-width apart, ensuring you feel stable in this position. Let your arms rest on your sides, and stand tall with your head up and your back straight.*

2. *Engage your core and breathe in sharply.*

3. *Raise your right leg to the knee level and point your toes outwards to create a 45-degree angle between your hips and toes. Keep breathing and hold this position without shifting the weight to the other leg.*

4. *Start rotating the leg clockwise and make 360 degrees, returning the portion to its original raised angle before turning it counter-clockwise to the same position. It would help if you did not bend your knees but anchor your body with your abs and hips.*

5. *Lower the right leg and perform the motion with your left leg, ensuring you make two 360-degree moves.*

Do this five times for each leg.

TIP:

Ensure you keep breathing as you rotate the legs, practicing deep breathing as explained under the Pilates principles.

DAY 3: WALL PUSH-UPS AND ARM CIRCLES

Wall Push-Ups

Pushing yourself off the wall may seem simple, but it is a great way to work your **triceps, pectoral muscles, and shoulders** for higher strength and endurance.

1. *Stand one arm's length away from the wall to ensure a 45-degree angle when you push yourself off the wall. Place your feet at shoulder width apart and rest your palms against the wall at shoulder height. Your arms should also be shoulder-width apart.*

2. *Inhale as you slowly lean towards the wall by bending your elbows without moving your feet or arching your back. Exercise control by counting to five so you do not tire or lose your balance.*

3. *Stop leaning in when your chest or chin touches the wall, and hold this position for two seconds.*

4. *Exhale as you slowly push yourself off the wall back to the original position. Count to two for safety.*

5. *Repeat this motion ten times for the first set, then rest for a minute. Then do it ten more times.*

Take your time to avoid injuries and ensure your muscles work hard enough for you to see and feel the results.

Arm Circles

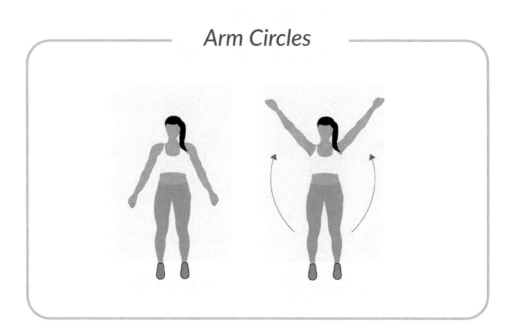

Arm circles are a great way to target your **shoulders, chest, and upper back.** They feature little yet effective movements:

1. *Place your feet firmly on the ground at shoulder-width distance. Raise your arms and extend them to the sides at a 90-degree angle. Keep them straight, and do not bend your elbows.*

2. *Breathe in and rotate the extended arms clockwise as you make big circles. You should feel the burn in your arms. Keep going at it as you breathe in and out, as explained in the Pilates principles. Please do this for twenty seconds, then change the direction to anticlockwise and keep at it for twenty more seconds.*

3. *Take a twenty-second break and repeat the exercise. Do this for five sets.*

Keep your core engaged, your back straight, and your arms extended. Also, keep the movements slow to ensure your muscles work hard.

DAY 4: PELVIC CURLS AND BRIDGE WITH WALL SUPPORT

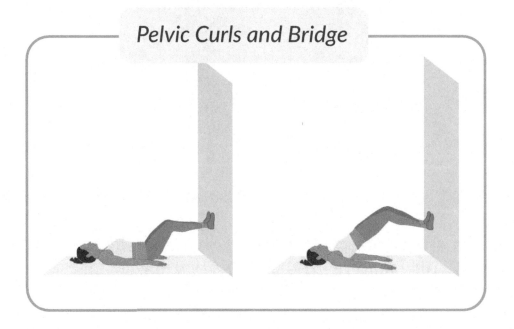

Pelvic Curls and Bridge

These movements target your **hamstrings, glutes, and abdominals.** By doing them on the wall, you enjoy more range of motion as follows:

1. *Lie flat on the floor or mat, ensuring your back is flat, with your knees bent at 45 degrees and your toes touching the wall.*

2. *Elevate your body by placing one foot against the wall two feet high*

and do the same for the other foot to create a 90-degree angle between the feet and knees.

3. *Keep your hands at your side with the palms facing down. Inhale and raise your legs and tailbone towards the ceiling. Then exhale and lift your lower back and hips as you roll your spine to settle between your shoulders. Do this from your upper to lower back.*

4. *Inhale and return to the original position.*

Do this ten times, taking a ten-second break between the exercises.

Pelvic Curls and Bridge

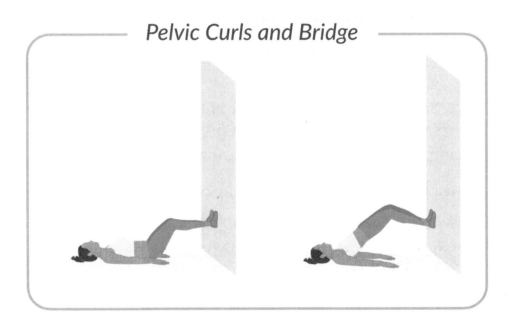

Glute bridges are similar to pelvic curls, targeting your **hamstrings, glutes, and abdominals.** But in the case of the glute bridge, your hamstrings and glutes work harder:

1. *Lie flat on the floor or mat, ensuring your back is flat, with your knees bent at 45 degrees and your toes touching the wall.*

2. *Elevate your body by placing one foot against the wall two feet high and do the same for the other foot to create a 90-degree angle between the feet and knees.*

3. *Keep your hands at your side with the palms facing down. Inhale and squeeze your glutes as you engage your core. Then exhale as you push your body towards the ceiling and squeeze your glutes. Your knees and neck should connect in a straight line. Hold this position for five seconds and slowly lower your body as you inhale and relax your glutes without relaxing your core.*

Do this ten times, taking a ten-second break between the exercises.

DAY 5: REST AND RECOVERY

You've had a few active days. Now is the time to let your body rest, as this optimizes muscle recovery, eases fatigue, and reduces the chances of injury. So, what's on the itinerary?

- *No exercise today – enjoy your day off,*
- *Hydrate with at least eight glasses of water, and*
- *Get enough sleep. Most people are okay with 6 to 8 hours.*

That's it for the day!

DAY 6: REVIEW AND REFLECT ON WEEK 1 PROGRESS

Tracking your progress is essential to helping you advance in Wall Pilates. Here's how you do it:

1. *Attempt the fitness assessment tests we covered in the previous chapter, i.e., the pushups, wall sits, and planks. Hold on for as long as you can.*

2. *Review your statistics. Have you improved? If so, where? Consider your progress in endurance, upper body strength, core strength, and lower body strength.*

These statistics will help you determine whether you're practicing Pilates principles as needed. For example, if you have engaged your core this week, you should do better at planks.

DAY 7: ACTIVE REST DAY

Now is the time to prepare for the coming week by gently stretching to warm up your muscles. You also get to practice what you have learned all week:

- *Do the wall roll down and spine stretch five times*
- *Rest for five seconds*
- *Do four wall squats*
- *Rest for ten seconds*
- *Do three leg circles for each leg*
- *Rest for fifteen seconds*
- *Do five wall pushups*
- *Rest for twenty seconds*
- *Do twenty-second arm circles for each arm*
- *Rest for twenty seconds*
- *Do five pelvic curls*

- *Rest for twenty seconds*
- *Do five glute bridges*

This workout should be about twenty minutes long. Do the exercises feel more manageable? You're making progress.

Week 2 – Enhancing Flexibility

The second week builds on the first one. Since we have worked on your strength, we can boost your flexibility by adding more movements to the program. These exercises will take about 20 to 25 minutes, and you can easily incorporate them into your schedule.

DAY 8: WALL ROLL DOWN WITH HIP OPENER

Wall roll-down stretch

We start with the wall roll down as we did in week 1 to target your **abs and shoulders** as follows:

1. *Stand next to a wall with your back to the wall, leaving about eight to ten inches of space between your body and the wall.*

2. *Plant your feet firmly on the ground and ensure you feel stable as you maintain a shoulder-width distance between your feet. Place your arms on your side and relax them so they fall against your torso.*

3. *Engage your core by pulling in your abs and relaxing your shoulders to ensure they do not touch your ears. Breathe in and feel the air as it pushes your diaphragm down and your rib cage out, resulting in a broad chest.*

4. *Start exhaling as you move your body downwards from the head to the spine. Feel as you move each vertebra as you push out the air*

forcefully. Ensure your core remains engaged as you do this so you can feel as the spine lengthens with each roll.

5. *Allow your arms to follow the movement parallel to your ears but ensure your hips remain against the wall. Do this slowly and feel as the tension releases from your body. Keep rolling down until you cannot do so without moving your hips.*

6. *Inhale at this point as you keep engaging your core and feel the effect. Focus on how your body feels from head to toe. You will likely get a good stretch even in your legs, but you should not feel pain.*

7. *Exhale sharply as you roll up, starting from your lower abs. It would help to use your hips and lower abs to hinge this motion to ensure you target one vertebra at a time. Rolling back up might prompt you to create tension in your shoulders but avoid doing this by relaxing them.*

8. *Come back to the original position without disengaging your abs.*

Repeat the exercise ten times.

Hip Openers

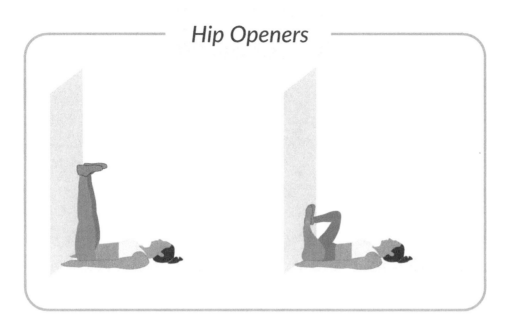

These exercises stretch the **hips and lower back**, relieving tension and pain and improving flexibility. Proceed as follows:

1. *Sit near the wall and lie on your back with your hands on your sides. Lift your legs and rest them on the wall, then slowly scoot your lower back towards the wall as you raise your legs further up. Keep breathing normally.*

2. *Once your butt touches the wall, stop moving toward it. Instead, straighten your feet against the wall such that they form a 90-degree angle with your upper body. Slowly bend your knees and bring your soles together so they touch. Keep breathing in this position as you feel your thighs and hips burn. After five breaths, relax your legs by raising them again to make a 90-degree angle. Rest for five seconds.*

Repeat this exercise five more times.

DAY 9: HAMSTRING STRETCHES WITH WALL ASSISTANCE

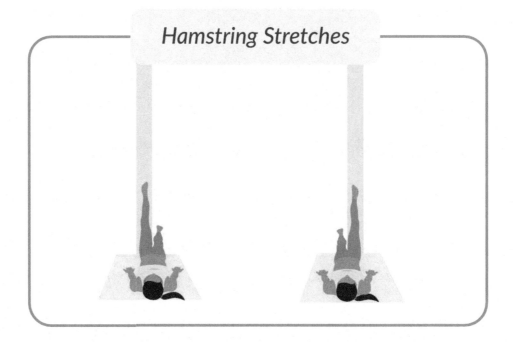

Hamstring Stretches

Hamstring stretches target the **hamstrings** and increase their flexibility by boosting the range of motion in the hips. They also alleviate lower back pain and improve your posture by flattening the natural back arch. You can perform them as follows:

1. *Find an outer wall corner or a door frame to have space to raise one leg while keeping the other lowered and straight.*

2. *Lift your right leg and bring its heel to rest against the wall while allowing a slight knee bend. Straighten your left leg through the door frame or open space and feel the stretch on the back of your thigh.*

3. *Hold this position for twenty seconds while practicing breath control, then switch the legs.*

4. *Repeat for twenty-two seconds and move closer to the wall. Keep repeating while adding two seconds until you get to thirty seconds.*

Give yourself a break, then repeat the exercise for two more sets.

DAY 10: WALL ANGELS AND THIGH SCULPTING EXERCISES

Wall angels

Wall angels target your **upper and lower back** for reduced tension, allowing you to experience a deep spine stretch, increasing mobility. Proceed as follows:

1. *Sit tall against a wall with your back pressed against the wall, ensuring even your arch pushes the wall. Breathe in and extend your legs in front for extra stability as you bring your elbows to the side at shoulder height.*

2. *Push your triceps against the wall and have your backs of hands pressing on the wall. Make a 90-degree angle with your elbows so that your arms face upward against the wall, yet your triceps are parallel to the ground.*

3. *Keep breathing as you raise your arms above your head so your arms face up and your elbows are fully extended. Do not stop pressing your back against the wall. Return to the original position with your triceps parallel to the ground.*

4. *Repeat this movement ten times and take a break.*

Complete five sets.

DAY 11: STANDING LEG STRETCHES WITH WALL SUPPORT

Standing leg stretches

These exercises target the **hip flexors and adductors** and boost flexibility significantly. They also stretch the spine and entire body, relieving tension.

1. *Face the wall with your feet together, maintaining a two-foot distance from the wall.*

2. *Lean towards the wall while keeping your body straight at the hips and knees. Raise your hands and let your arms rest on the wall in this raised position such that you feel the stretch from tip to toe. Hold this position for ten seconds, breathing per the deep breathing technique.*

3. *Return to the original position and rest for thirty seconds. Repeat the exercise by adding 5-second increments until you get to forty seconds. Then start from 10 seconds and repeat the entire set.*

Do not strain your body. Instead, stretch only as far as your body will allow.

DAY 12: REST AND RECOVERY

You deserve some time off from active workouts. Take this day off to recover. Eat nutritious foods, hydrate, sleep enough, and enjoy time doing what you want, e.g., hanging out with your friends. Sustainability is the goal, and you can't achieve this without adequate rest.

DAY 13: REVIEW AND REFLECT ON WEEK 2 PROGRESS

Today's review will be more involving as it features last week's progress measured against your initial stats and week 2's results. Proceed as follows:

1. *Attempt the fitness assessment tests in Chapter 3 and record your results.*

2. *Contrast the results with week 1's progress and your initial results. Can you see any changes? Are you getting better?*

Record your results as you will use them to gauge your week three progress. You should have a much better experience with the tests due to added mobility by the end of week 2.

DAY 14: ACTIVE REST DAY

- *Do the wall roll down and spine stretch five times*
- *Rest for five seconds*
- *Do five hip openers*
- *Rest for five seconds*
- *Do a set of hamstring stretches*
- *Rest for ten seconds*
- *Do a set of wall angels*
- *Rest for ten seconds*
- *Do a set of standing leg stretches.*

Week 3 – Building Strength and Balance

Are you ready for more robust planks and pushups? This week will have you improving your previous stats. You need to carve out 30 to 35 minutes per workout.

DAY 15: WALL TEASER AND ABDOMINAL EXERCISES

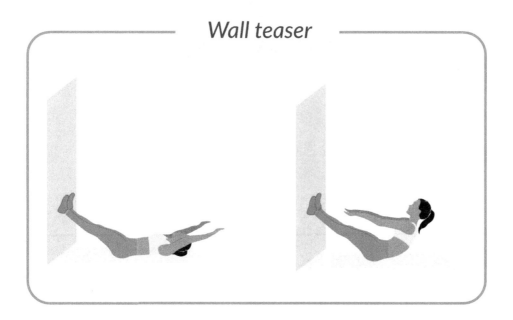

Wall teaser

Wall teasers require you to practice core engagement, precision, and breath control.

1. *Lie flat on the floor with your back flat and hurry up to the wall. Place your legs at a 45-degree angle and keep them straight.*

2. *Raise and straighten your arms and bring them towards the back of your head. Then, with your feet firmly on the wall, raise your hands and upper body and linger your hands over the elevated legs with your upper body at a 45-degree angle with the legs. Stop when you feel like you cannot move anymore. You will feel your abs burning at this point.*

3. *Breathe and hold this position for ten seconds. Then slowly lower your upper body hands to the original post.*

4. *Repeat the process with 5-second increments until you can hold the position for twenty seconds.*

Do ten sets, ensuring you breathe correctly each time.

DAY 16: WALL EXTENSIONS AND SPINE STRENGTHENING

Spine Strengthening

Your thoracic spine requires stretching for mobility and strength, which allows you to progress to other Pilates exercises. Stretching also improves core control and stability.

1. *Stand with your face to the wall with your feet together.*

2. *Lean forward while hinging your hips until you can create a 90-degree angle between your hips and the tips of your hands. Ensure your palms are flat against the wall. Stretch your body by maintaining firm feet and your hands on the wall. Have your hands slightly elevated at a 30-degree angle but keep your upper body parallel to the ground.*

3. *Inhale and exhale in this position with your face facing down for ten seconds. Then arch your back, raise your hands to reach as far as they can, and hold this position. Keep breathing for ten seconds.*

4. *Return to the original position and repeat the exercise five times.*

Rest for a minute. Then redo the exercise in five more sets, each with 5-second increments. The last set should have 35-second holds. Do not strain your back or legs while arching or stretching your spine.

DAY 17: SIDE LEG LIFTS AND CORE ACTIVATION

Side leg lifts

The side leg lift targets your **abs, hamstrings, and glutes.** And you will feel the burn as you lower and raise your legs while maintaining a balance. Here's how you do it against a wall:

1. *Lie on your side next to a wall with one leg on top of the other while keeping your legs straight. Then elevate your body by resting your upper body on your elbow, which you should bend at a 45-degree angle such that your shoulder lies directly above it. Place your other arm on the hip facing the ceiling.*

2. *Engage your core and exhale as you raise the upper leg towards the ceiling without moving it forward or back. Use the wall to stabilize your back as you hold the elevated position for two seconds. Slowly lower the leg, using your core to maintain control, and rest the shank on the lower one. Repeat this exercise five times, then change your position such that you now elevate the lower leg. Do this for five moves.*

3. *Return to the original position and rest for a minute. Then do five more reps.*

Exercise core control to ensure the movements are slow to avoid injury and to put enough pressure on the muscles.

DAY 18: WALL PUSH-UP VARIATIONS

Push-Up

Wall push-ups are great for your **triceps, pectoral muscles, and shoulders** and can help you improve your endurance and strength. Here is how you should do this exercise:

1. *Stand one arm's length away from the wall to ensure a 45-degree angle when you push yourself off the wall. Place your feet at shoulder width apart and rest your palms against the wall at shoulder height. Your arms should also be shoulder-width apart.*

2. *Inhale as you slowly lean towards the wall by bending your elbows without moving your feet or arching your back. Exercise control by counting to five so you do not tire or lose your balance.*

3. *Stop leaning in when your chest or chin touches the wall, and hold this position for two seconds.*

4. *Exhale as you slowly push yourself off the wall back to the original position. Count to two for safety.*

5. *Repeat this motion ten times for the first set, then rest for a minute. Then do it ten more times.*

Variations

Test your progress since the first week by incorporating the following variations in the sets:

- *Increase the distance between your feet and the wall by five inches. That forces your body to work harder. Perform a set. Increase the distance by ten inches and do a group. Then add five more inches and complete one set.*

- *Reduce the distance between your hands such that you tuck your elbows at your sides. Complete a set.*

- *Use one arm, which you should center at half the distance of the original arm positioning to support your whole body. Complete one group, then change to the other hand and do the same.*

How does that feel?

DAY 19: REST AND RECOVERY

Let your muscles recover. Now is an excellent time to prep your meals, drink more water, soak in sunlight, take stock of your overall well-being, and sleep more.

DAY 20: REVIEW AND REFLECT ON WEEK 3 PROGRESS

Are you making progress? There is one easy way to find out.

1. *Complete the Chapter 3 fitness tests and record your stats. How long is your wall sit? How many push-ups can you do?*

2. *Compare the results with your initial, week 1, and week two results. Are there changes?*

By now, you should notice more endurance and strength. You have even moved to excellent wall sits. Even if you have room to go, we have a week to fine-tune those stats!

DAY 21: ACTIVE REST DAY

- *Do three sets of wall teasers*
- *Rest for ten seconds*
- *Do three sets of the wall extension*
- *Rest for ten seconds*
- *Do five side leg lifts per leg*
- *Rest for ten seconds*

- Perform a set of each wall push-up variation with a fifteen-second break between sets Week 4, here we come!

Week 4 - Mastering Control

By the start of this week, you should already feel a difference in your body. Your breath control, precision, core engagement, and alignment will have improved. And we can now work on exercises that require more power. These exercises will run for 35 to 40 minutes per workout.

DAY 22: FULL BODY INTEGRATION WITH WALL SUPPORT

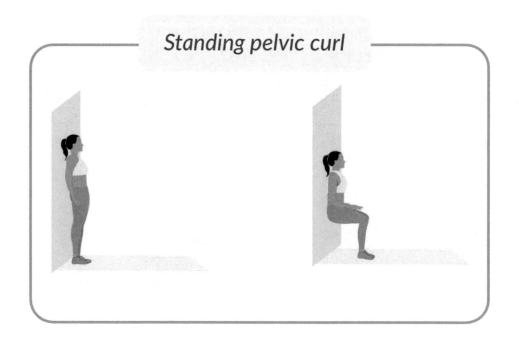

Standing pelvic curl

This exercise targets your **abs, glutes, and hamstrings** and is a variation of the standard wall sit.

1. *Stand next to a wall leaving about a two-foot distance between your back and the wall. Keeping your feet shoulder-width apart, picture an imaginary chair and start sliding down the wall to sit on it.*

2. *Push your back against the wall, ensuring your neck and lower back are straight with no arch. Keep sliding down until your hips are at a 90-degree angle with your knees.*

3. *Place your hands against the wall with your palms on the surface. Engage your core and lift your pelvis towards the ceiling without shifting your feet or upper back. You should feel the burn in your quadriceps, back, and abs. Hold this position for two seconds, then return to the starting position. Ensure you exhale as you lift and inhale as you return.*

4. *If the exercise feels too challenging, you can slide up the wall to lower the tension in your thighs. Repeat this set ten times and take a 30-second break.*

Do nine more sets.

Wall Pivot

This exercise stretches your **upper body, abs, and hamstrings** and is a great way to relieve the tension from standing pelvic curls.

1. *Stand straight a few inches from the wall with your feet shoulder-width apart. Breathe deeply and engage your core as you touch your hips.*

2. *Breathe as you lower your upper body and hinge it with your hips. As you do this, focus on controlling your body so that your upper body remains straight. Hold the pivot position for two seconds.*

3. *Inhale as you come back to the starting position. Then exhale as you pivot again, enjoying a full range of motion.*

4. *Do ten reps of this motion and take a one-minute break.*

Then do five more reps.

Wall Bird Dogs

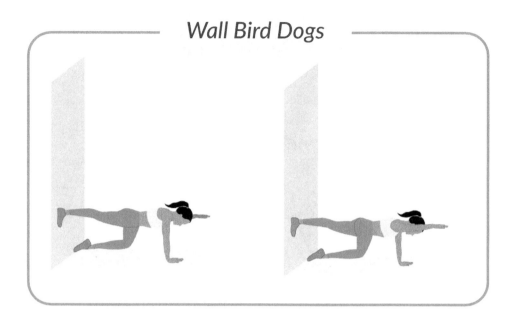

These exercises target your **core, arms, and thighs** and are a great way to exercise balance, control, and precision.

1. *Get on all fours facing away from the wall. Lift your right leg parallel to the floor and allow it to touch the wall. Only the ball of your foot should touch the wall – your heel should not. You should adjust yourself to find this position.*

2. *Ensure your left knee is on the floor at a right angle to the body and your arms are directly below your shoulders. In this position, engage your core and exhale as you lift your right leg a few inches above the wall and hold this position for two seconds.*

3. *Inhale and return to the starting position and repeat the exercise five times. Do the same with your left leg.*

4. *For the next set, lift your right leg and straighten your left arm so they are parallel to the ground. Exhale as you lift your right leg, but keep your arm similar. Do this five times, then alternate the legs and arms such that you raise your left leg and right arm.*

Do five more sets.

DAY 23: WALL HANDSTANDS AND BALANCE CHALLENGES

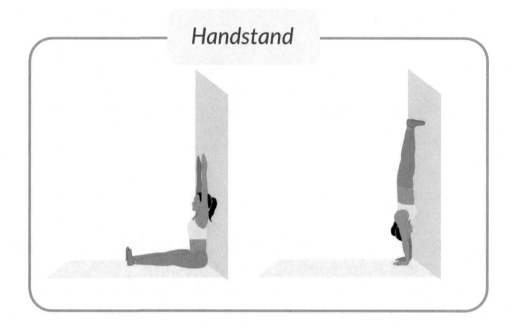

Handstand

Handstands are ideal for improving **upper body strength and balance.** However, doing them freestyle can be challenging and dangerous. Luckily, wall handstands transfer most of the weight off your hands and neck to ease the workout:

1. *Sit with your back against the wall and straighten your legs, ensuring you create a 90-degree angle at your waist. Then raise your hands above your head.*

2. *Tuck your legs and kneel on the ground. Then get on all fours facing away from the wall with your feet soles pressing against the wall and place your hands where your heels were.*

3. *Ensure your arms are straight and directly below your shoulders, and spread your fingers for more balance. Then pull your shoulders back.*

4. *If you feel stable, push your butt into the air such that you straighten your arms and legs and spread your feet against the wall.*

5. *Slowly start walking up the wall with your feet as you use your hands for support. Lift one foot to your hip height, then lift the other too. Keep breathing as you do this.*

6. *Start walking further up the wall as you move your hands closer to the wall for balance. Do this until you are parallel to the wall. Hold this position for ten seconds, then walk away from the wall by walking your hands away and slowly lowering your feet.*

7. *Get to the starting position, rest for a minute, and attempt another handstand.*

8. *If you cannot get parallel to the wall, doing a 90-degree angle, handstand will also work your entire body. You can attempt this for the first few tries until you feel ready for a complete handstand.*

Do ten handstands, ensuring you move slowly and not compromise your safety.

DAY 24: ADVANCED WALL EXERCISES FOR FLEXIBILITY AND STRENGTH

Split squat

This exercise targets your core, **glutes, and hamstrings**:

1. *Stand two feet away from the wall with your feet together. Slightly lean forward with your hands on your hips. Then push your right leg back such that your foot touches the base of the wall.*

2. *Get into a slight squat by bending your left leg and lowering your body as you exhale. Hold this position for two seconds, then inhale as you return to the starting point. Do this ten times, ensuring you control your movements and not allow your knee to go over your toes.*

3. *Alternate your legs so that you bend your right leg while your left leg is against the wall. Do this ten times.*

4. *Take a one-minute break, then do four more sets.*

The lower you go, the more you work your muscles, increasing endurance and strength.

Forward Stretch

This exercise targets your **core, hamstrings, glutes, and upper body:**

1. *Stand two feet from the wall with your feet together. Push your right leg back so the heel rests on the wall, yet your football is on the floor.*

2. *Move your left leg forward to create a wide angle between your feet. Put your hands on your side raised and slightly lean forward with a straight upper body.*

3. *Exhale as you push your body forward and bend your left leg forward without bending your right leg. Hold this position for two seconds and return to the original starting point as you inhale.*

4. *Do this ten times while practicing core engagement and breath control.*

5. *Switch the legs and do the exercise ten more times.*

Rest for a minute, then do nine more sets.

DAY 25: DYNAMIC WALL MOVEMENTS AND COORDINATION

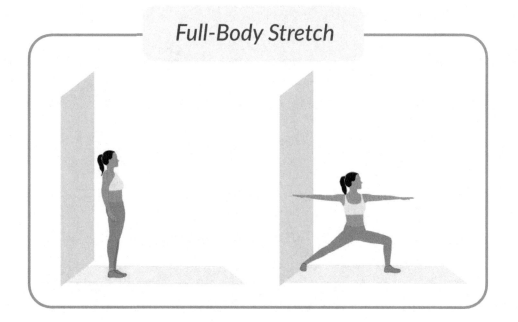

Full-Body Stretch

This movement targets your **glutes, hamstrings, core, and arms:**

1. *Stand two feet from the wall with your feet together. Push your right leg back so the heel rests on the wall, yet your football is on the floor.*

2. *Move your left leg forward to create a wide angle between your feet. Put your hands on your side parallel to your upper body and slightly lean forward with a straight upper body.*

3. *Exhale as you bend your left leg forward without bending your right leg to create a 90-degree angle.*

4. *Keeping your upper body straight, move your arms parallel to the ground. Then exhale and lift them to face the ceiling while engaging your core. Inhale and return them to a similar position.*

5. *Do this ten times, then switch the legs for ten more movements.*

6. *Take a one-minute break before doing four more sets.*

The lower you are, the better the workout.

Full-Body Twist

This exercise engages your core, hips, upper body, and glutes. You will feel the burn.

1. *Stand two feet from the wall with your feet together. Push your right leg back so the heel rests on the wall, yet your foot ball is on the floor.*

2. *Move your left leg forward to create a wide angle between your feet. Put your hands on your side parallel to your upper body and slightly lean forward with a straight upper body.*

3. *Exhale as you bend your left leg forward without bending your right leg to create a 90-degree angle.*

4. *Keeping your upper body straight, move your arms parallel to the ground. Then open your arms to create a 180-degree angle such that they are on opposite sides. Exhale and rotate your body at a 90-degree angle to the left without altering your leg positions. Hold this position for two seconds and inhale, then turn to the right as you exhale.*

5. *Do this ten times, then change your legs so your right leg is forward and your left leg provides wall support. Do the exercise ten more times.*

6. *Rest for two minutes and do five more sets.*

Keep your body low for slow controlled movements.

DAY 26: REST AND RECOVERY

It's rest day! Use this time to appreciate your body and everything it can do. Sleep, cook your favorite dish, get a massage, lather your body in oils, do some journaling – whatever makes you happy. Remember to hydrate!

DAY 27: REVIEW AND REFLECT ON WEEK 4 PROGRESS

Four weeks of Wall Pilates will have a positive impact on anyone. You can expect your stats to have improved. Here's how you know:

1. *Go through the fitness tests in Chapter 3 and record your scores. How are your pushups? What about your wall sits and planks?*

2. *Compare your week 4 results and initial scores to the past three weeks. What has changed?*

3. *Review the goals you set in Chapter 3. Have you achieved them?*

This progress marks the start of a lifetime. So, even if you are not where you want to be, pat yourself.

DAY 28: FINAL CHALLENGE - FULL PILATES WALL WORKOUT SEQUENCE

What's a fitness program without a test that helps you review your performance? This sequence will comprise all the workouts you have done since day 1 and will take forty minutes. Let's do this!

- *Do five wall roll-downs*
- *Rest for ten seconds*
- *Do five wall squats with 5-second holds and two leg circles per leg*
- *Rest for ten seconds*
- *Do five wall push-ups and three arm circles per hand*
- *Rest for ten seconds*
- *Do five pelvic curls*
- *Rest for twenty seconds*
- *Do five wall roll-downs and five hip openers*
- *Rest for ten seconds*
- *Do five hamstring stretches and five wall angels*
- *Rest for ten seconds*

- *Do five standing leg stretches and five wall teasers*
- *Rest for twenty seconds*
- *Do five wall extensions and two side leg lifts per leg*
- *Rest for ten seconds*
- *Do two reps of each wall push-up variation*
- *Rest for twenty seconds*
- *Do five standing pelvic curls and five wall pivots*
- *Rest for ten seconds*
- *Do five wall bird dogs*
- *Rest for twenty seconds*
- *Do one handstand*
- *Rest for twenty seconds*
- *Do two split squats, forward stretches, and full-body stretches per leg*
- *Rest for twenty seconds*
- *Do five full-body twists per leg*

You're done! And you can start from week 1 again to practice the Pilates moves even more.

CHAPTER 5:
EXERCISE CHART AND STRATEGIES FOR SELF-CONTROL AND EXPERT ADVICE AND TIPS FOR SUCCESS

In Chapter 3, I mentioned the need for clear goals on why you are embarking on this Wall Pilates journey. The goals help you stay on track and push through days when showing up feels like a lot of work. This chapter enables you to visualize your journey and arms you with expert advice on making it through the challenge.

The Exercise Chart

Chapter 4 breaks down the steps in all the exercises, aiding you in practicing the core Pilates principles. Even so, picturing the road ahead can be challenging when you have no idea where you're headed. The exercise chart on the next page helps you understand what you need to do each day.

Moreover, you can use it to modify your Wall Pilates workouts once you have finished the challenge. E.g., you can do wall push-ups and arm circles on day 1 and perform wall squats and leg circles the next day. But for the first attempt at the challenge, use the workouts as shown to ensure you build your endurance gradually.

You can print the chart page and use it as a reference during and after the challenge.

The 28-Day Wall Pilates Challenge

	Day 1	Day 2	Day 3	Day 4	Day 5	Day 6	Day 7
Week 1	Wall Roll-Down and Spine Stretch	Wall Squats Leg Circles	Wall Push-Ups Arm Circles	Pelvic Curls Glute Bridges	Rest and Recovery	Review and Reflect on Week 1 Progress	Active Rest Day
Week 2	Wall Roll Downs Hip Openers	Hamstring Stretches	Wall Angels	Standing Leg Stretches	Rest and Recovery	Review and Reflect on Week 2 Progress	Active Rest Day
Week 3	Wall Teaser	Wall Extensions	Side Leg Lifts	Wall Push-Up Variations	Rest and Recovery	Review and Reflect on Week 3 Progress	Active Rest Day
Week 4	Standing Pelvic Curl Wall Pivot Wall Bird Dogs	Wall Hand-stands	The Split Squat Forward Stretch	The Full-Body Stretch Full-Body Twist	Rest and Recovery	Review and Reflect on Week 4 Progress	Active Rest Day

Avoiding Core Mistakes in Wall Pilates

As seen from the 28-day challenge walkthrough, doing Wall Pilates is manageable. Even people who barely work out can get the hang of things. It comes down to following the instructions, engaging your core, and breathing correctly. As such, you must avoid the common mistakes below as these can injure you, tire you more than necessary, or even turn a fun workout into a chore:

a. *Not warming up: As stated in Chapter 3, you must warm up before any routine. You can do this by jogging on the spot, doing light stretching, or even walking. Do this for five minutes; your joints will be prone to straining, especially if you lead a sedentary life.*

b. *Not resting: I have included rest days each week coupled with active recovery days. You may think you can get more out of the challenge by working out on rest days. But that only strains your muscles as they do not get enough time to recover. Take time off for the good of your body.*

c. *Not eating right: Undereating, overeating, and not balancing your macros are common mistakes when exercising. The next chapter covers how you can have your cake and eat it without compromising your performance.*

d. *Not practicing consistency: The review stages in all the weeks should show upward progress if you stick to the program. Thus, you will likely not see changes if you start skipping days. Skipping workouts when you are sick or have unavoidable reasons is okay. But if nothing is amiss, keep to the schedule to improve your performance and results.*

e. *Not hydrating enough: I have mentioned hydration often in the workouts. But is taking fluids that necessary? Of course! Water is*

essential in cooling your body, transporting nutrients, and supporting overall bodily functions. With it, your performance can improve. Don't wait till you feel thirsty to drink water – thirst is a sign of dehydration.

f. *Not sleeping enough: Your muscles need to recover. And when you sleep, they get time to do this as your body repairs itself. Sleeping also helps you deal with fitness-related fatigue to show up in good form. You should aim to get at least seven hours of sleep each night.*

g. *Training too much: The 28-day challenge starts slowly before picking up pace. You should take your time with the process by attempting two days in one day. Doing this stresses your body, and instead of seeing results faster, you will likely tire or hurt your muscles. Kindly stick to the program and trust the process.*

h. *Not following the steps: Each exercise has a detailed breakdown of the instructions. Following the steps allows you to maintain proper form and avoid getting injured. Ensure you use the instructions to perform any move.*

Your fitness journey is a marathon and not a sprint. And the only way to make it sustainable and enjoyable is to take it easy and only push yourself per your level. Avoid making the mistakes above, and everything else will fall into place. Trust me - 28 days are enough to make a huge difference!

Ditching Motivation for Discipline: Staying Consistent

Here is the thing. Motivation is a great tool to get you started on any venture, be it exercise, business, or even a relationship. But it's not enough to fuel the whole journey. Many people start exercising with a lot of motivation. But along the way, they veer off the track as they fall into old habits. The best way to stick to any program is discipline. Motivation gets you started, and a sentence gets you there.

Here are five strategies that work for my clients:

1. *Be clear about your goal: Discipline will only help if your goals are wise. You should know what you want when you want it and how you can get it. This goal informs your action steps. You can use Chapter 3 to refresh your memory on setting your goals.*

2. *Understand why your goal matters: A purposeless goal is less motivating than one that ties to your WHY. Why do you want to achieve the goal? For example, you should build your endurance to hike more. Whenever you question why you're sticking to a schedule, you will remember WHY and feel motivated to keep going.*

3. *Outline your challenges: Changes take work to implement. Think about all the hurdles you will face as you start this new challenge, e.g., carving out 20 minutes for a workout, not believing in yourself, etc. Be honest with yourself; this will help you develop sound mitigation measures. For example, you can use positive affirmations to get you through days when you feel your life cannot improve.*

4. *Out with the old and in with the new: Your mitigation measures will help you replace the old habits that have held you back. For example, if you spend your evenings scrolling social media, you can use that time to do a workout and prep your meals. These seemingly complex things will soon become a part of your life you enjoy. And instead of seeing them as inconveniences, you will start embracing them as productive activities once you start seeing and feeling the changes.*

5. *Track your progress: Ensure that your SMART goal has KPIs that you can use to measure how far you have come. Tracking enables you to gauge what you have done, which informs you where you have improved or stalled. It also helps you understand when it's time to increase your goals. For example, if you have been growing your push-ups by five weekly for a month, try aiming for ten a week.*

Consistency is not natural to most people. But the good thing is that you can cultivate this significant value by having a goal and sticking to the plan. I'd be lying if I said having motivation was the only way through!

CHAPTER 6: PROPER NUTRITION FOR WOMEN AND SENIORS

You cannot outrun a bad diet!

Many people start exercise programs that keep what they eat the same. But guess what? Such efforts often fail because 80% of your nutrition accounts for your success. So, if you mainly eat what people like calling "empty calories," your results won't be as good as those of someone who eats healthier foods. Why?

– *Calorie-dense foods, e.g., pizzas and burgers, only satisfy your hunger for a while. So, they spike your blood sugar levels and leave you feeling full, but this only lasts a short time. Eventually, you feel hungry and start looking for more food, thus exceeding your maintenance calories.*

– *Calorie-dense foods have fewer nutrients than nutrient-dense foods. So, your body barely gets its minimum requirements, which affects your performance. Vitamins and minerals are crucial to any diet, and lacking them affects your overall well-being and can result in nutrient-deficient-related illnesses.*

– *Calorie-dense foods often negatively impact hormones. Please note that this happens when you consume them in large amounts. These foods affect your weight, hormone regulation, and brain activity. Prolonged overconsumption of these foods can thus deteriorate your health.*

So, what's the answer? Does this mean you must follow a strict diet? Not at all. As I said, this book is about sustainability. I don't expect you to lead a life where eating a cookie sends you spiraling. I want you to have your cake, eat it, and maybe add some kale! Let's find the balance!

Using Food as Fuel through Intuitive Eating

Food is fuel. After all, calories are fuel stored in food. When you consume more energy than your body needs, it keeps it fat. And when you consume less energy than you need, your body breaks down to account for the deficit. Thus, anyone who wants to lose weight has a calorie deficit, those who wish to maintain their weight eat at maintenance calories, and those who want to gain weight eat a surplus. But what kind of food should you eat and how should you eat?

Usually, people make healthy lifestyles unattainable. You may have even been on a diet that made your life miserable as it had you eating foods you did not want. Or worse – it had you undereating, so you were always hungry (hungry and angry). Such diets are not only bad for your physical health but also for your mental well-being. Moreover, many of them fail because they are too rigid.

Does that mean you should not diet? Of course not! Anything you eat is a diet. You can be on a diet of pizzas and bagels or one of radishes and water. All food constitutes a diet. So, consider a lifestyle change instead of feeling your foods a good or bad diet. Stop thinking of food as the enemy and instead embrace it as fuel using the principles below:

1. *Eat when hungry: Your signals indicate that your body needs fuel. Please do not ignore them. Instead, find food and satisfy that cue.*

2. *Stop eating when complete: Do you often finish all the food on your plate even when complete? Stop doing that. Instead, stop eating when you have enjoyed a meal and feel full. You can always resume when you feel hungry.*

3. *Eat regular meals: I often encourage my clients to eat five to six times daily. Doing this helps them maintain their blood sugar levels. It also helps them avoid moments where they feel ravenous.*

4. *Reach for healthy options: Nutrient-dense foods leave you feeling fuller for longer. Prioritize vegetables, fruits, proteins, and carbs. Most calories should come from whole grains, lean meats, fruits, and leafy vegetables. Of course, you can always add calorie-dense foods to your diet.*

5. *Eat foods you enjoy: A common reason behind overeating is that people eat foods that do not satisfy their taste hunger. Find ways to make your cooking taste better. Or order in foods you love. When you do this, you find yourself eating less than usual.*

6. *Stop labeling foods as good or bad: My clients often come in, thinking I will tell them to avoid certain foods, e.g., soda. But I do off foods. Instead, I encourage moderation. For example, if you enjoy cakes, you can make room for cakes in your diet, even daily! But most calories should come from nutrient-dense foods with longer-lasting energy effects and more nutrients.*

7. *Avoid emotional eating: Many people use food as a coping mechanism, e.g., for boredom, sadness, or anger. But instead of using food, try other helpful tactics, e.g., stretching, reading books, watching movies, talking to a friend, etc.*

8. *Drink enough fluids: Water is a great way to stay hydrated. But teas, coffee, juices, milk, and other liquids have high hydration indices. You can use them to reach your hydration goal: at least eight glasses of fluids each day. Ideally, it should be water. But whatever gets you there!*

9. *Track your calorie intake: Knowing what you eat helps you understand your food intake better. For example, if your maintenance calories are 2,000 and you want to lose weight, you should <2,000 calories daily. Tracking helps you understand what you have eaten and how it affects your goal.*

What does a sustainable eating lifestyle look like?

- You can eat out with your friends without worrying about what is on the menu,

- You can turn down food when you are not hungry or if it does not meet your taste preferences,

- You can use food to fuel your body, e.g., eating more proteins to build lean muscle for better performance,

- You enjoy food and look at it as a source of fuel and not a coping mechanism,

- You eat both nutrient-dense and calorie-dense foods and practice moderation to avoid feeling restricted or binging, and

- You eat in a way you can maintain ten years from now.

If your diet leaves you feeling restricted, sad, or even angry, you will have difficulty sticking to it. I will not share a meal plan with you as I want you to feel free when making the right food choices for your body. It would help if you did not think that you have to start your day with an oatmeal smoothie or end your day with a protein shake. Go with the flow, track your calories, and focus more on nutrient-dense options.

Parting Shot

Also, consider fixing your relationship with food by seeking therapy. I advocate working with a registered dietician who can help you work through your feelings.

TIP:

1. Find a balanced dietician.

2. Avoid dieticians who are too rigid, as they will severely restrict the foods you love.

3. On the same note, avoid those who tell you you can eat whatever you like whenever you want; the consequences do not matter.

There is a balance between the two, which is healthy for you physically and mentally. And like the entire book reiterates, moderation is SUSTAINABLE!

CHAPTER 7: CONCLUSION

Have you shied away from working out before? Many people have. After all, the challenges to fitness bar many people from leading active lives, especially those with safety concerns. Nobody wants to walk into a gym and get pushed to the point of feeling sick, frustrated, or even sad. Seeing people crying in the gym has almost become standard. And you will see a trainer shouting at them to keep going because the pain is worth it. But is it? Most people who go through such challenges often stop working out because they start thinking of working out as:

- *Hard,*

- *Costly,*

- *Time-consuming,*

- *Unsustainable, etc.*

But giving up is not the answer – Nor is being part of any program that makes you dread working out. The trick lies in finding a program that anyone can enjoy regardless of their fitness level, financial capacity, time considerations, or preferences. And Wall Pilates offers the perfect replacement for all other costly, time-consuming, and challenging workouts. You don't need to know how to burpee or scale a wall in ten seconds. You don't even need to be a fitness expert. You can start Wall Pilates as you are and with what you have. And you only need a wall!

The Beauty of Wall Pilates

Wall Pilates builds on traditional Pilates workouts and helps you build endurance, strength, and flexibility while restoring your correct posture. And you do this by relying on the core Pilates principles:

breath control, alignment, core engagement, and balance. Once you have mastered these basics, progressing to traditional Pilates becomes easier. And the best part? Wall Pilates is so effective that you can keep following the workouts and getting a good workout like conventional Pilates. Many of my clients have enjoyed the activities so much that they opted to stick to Pilates on the wall. And how could they not? The exercises are:

- **Safe** – *maintaining balance and control is easy with the wall backing you. And that's why this exercise is a good choice for older adults, women, and people with special safety considerations.*

- **Cheap** – *unlike traditional workouts that require machines and accessories, you can start Wall Pilates without anything besides a wall. And I'm sure you can find a wall to start your progress.*

- **Customizable** – *once you get the hang of Wall Pilates, you can change the program to fit your needs. And you can also practice other exercises on the wall.*

Most importantly, Wall Pilates is a sustainable workout program. It does not require you to go out of your way to start. You don't need to buy fancy gear or clothes or get on any strict diets. It allows you to build a sustainable lifestyle as your life does not revolve around workouts. Instead, the exercises are just part of your healthy lifestyle.

Staying on Track

While Wall Pilates is arguably one of the most manageable workouts, your progress depends on your adherence to your goals. It would help if you started with clear SMART goals, as I have outlined in the third chapter. Sticking to it is easy when you know what you want from any program. Is it more endurance? Do you want to lose weight? Whatever it is, you must keep it in mind and build your KPIs towards reaching it.

Finishing the 28-Day Challenge will help you start a new and sustainable healthy lifestyle. As I said, this new journey is a marathon; you should take joy in the journey, not the destination. As you progress in your wall workouts, you will see the apparent transformation and feel it in how you relate to your body, food, and life in general.

I have included a workout log on the next page to help you track your progress every 14 days, even after the 28-Day program, including active and rest days. You can print a new leaf after 14 days or input your progress using an online pen to erase each week's progress and start again. *(You can leave out the weight if that's not your KPI and include something else, like an endurance test using wall sits. There is no hard and fast rule regarding KPIs, and you can choose one per your goal.)*

Date	Workout	Sets	Reps	Weight

Logging your progress encourages you to stay consistent even when old habits start kicking in. Here are other ways to ensure you impart wall workouts in your healthy lifestyle without losing sight of what's important:

– *Start with a SMART goal – I cannot emphasize this enough. You can measure it over time, e.g., building strength or losing weight.*

– *Understand the purpose of your goal. Most people aim to feel better, move better, and increase their quality of life. What's yours?*

– *Find a great way to track your progress, e.g., using the workout log above.*

– *Replace your old habits with better ones aligned with your goal, and*

– *Remain disciplined even when things seem complicated.*

Motivation, as I said, is a fantastic way to get started on anything. But once challenges rear their heads, motivation can dwindle. On the other hand, discipline remains decisive regarding the willingness to keep going even when the excuses seem to make sense. Remember why you started this journey, where you want to go, and what it means to you if you stop along the way.

The Way Forward

Working out does not have to be monotonous, costly, or a fleeting experience (like a fad diet). It can be an exciting activity that helps you work on your mind, body, and soul. And what better way to do this than with Wall Pilates? This workout is safe, cheap, fun, and sustainable. And if you have a wall, you have everything you need to get started. Write down your SMART goals, prepare for the program by understanding the Pilates principles, find a suitable wall, and start this exciting adventure.

That's how simple working out can be! If you found this helpful book, please leave a review on Amazon. If you are yet to finish the program, please do so – I would love your honest feedback on how you felt after making this integral life change.

Keep Going: You've got this!

Printed in Great Britain
by Amazon